PIANO ACCOMPANIMENT

first solo album

for violin

with piano accompaniment

Compiled, Arranged, and Edited
by HARVEY S. WHISTLER and HERMAN A. HUMMEL

CONTENTS

		PAGE NUMBERS	
		Solo Part	Piano Part
AUTUMN NOCTURNE	Harvey S. Whistler	3	4
CHRISTMAS SERENADE	Arr. Whistler-Hummel	10	18
CLOWN DANCE	Herman A. Hummel	11	20
CRADLE SONG (Wiegenlied) Op. 11, No. 2	Miska Hauser	9	16
EVENING BELLS	Herman A. Hummel	5	8
IN A CLOCK STORE	Charles J. Orth	7	12
ON WINGS OF SONG	Felix Mendelssohn	8	14
PRINCE CHARMING RONDO, Op. 123, No. 4	Charles Dancla	6	10
STARLIGHT WALTZ	Harvey S. Whistler	2	2
THEME AND VARIATION Op. 123, No. 7	Charles Dancla	12	22
TO A WILD ROSE from Woodland Sketches, Op. 51, No. 1 Edward MacDowell		4	6

RUBANK®

HAL•LEONARD®
CORPORATION
7777 W. BLUEMOUND RD. P.O. BOX 13819 MILWAUKEE, WI 53213

Starlight Waltz

HARVEY S. WHISTLER

4

Autumn Nocturne

HARVEY S. WHISTLER

To A Wild Rose
from Woodland Sketches

EDWARD MacDOWELL
Op. 51, No. 1

Evening Bells

HERMAN A. HUMMEL

Prince Charming
RONDO

CHARLES DANCLA
Op. 123, No. 4

In A Clock Store

CHARLES J. ORTH

VIOLIN PART

first solo album

for violin

with piano accompaniment

Compiled, Arranged, and Edited
by HARVEY S. WHISTLER and HERMAN A. HUMMEL

CONTENTS

		PAGE NUMBERS	
		Solo Part	Piano Part
AUTUMN NOCTURNE	Harvey S. Whistler	3	4
CHRISTMAS SERENADE	Arr. Whistler-Hummel	10	18
CLOWN DANCE	Herman A. Hummel	11	20
CRADLE SONG (Wiegenlied) Op. 11, No. 2	Miska Hauser	9	16
EVENING BELLS	Herman A. Hummel	5	8
IN A CLOCK STORE	Charles J. Orth	7	12
ON WINGS OF SONG	Felix Mendelssohn	8	14
PRINCE CHARMING RONDO, Op. 123, No. 4	Charles Dancla	6	10
STARLIGHT WALTZ	Harvey S. Whistler	2	2
THEME AND VARIATION Op. 123, No. 7	Charles Dancla	12	22
TO A WILD ROSE from Woodland Sketches, Op. 51, No. 1 Edward MacDowell		4	6

HAL•LEONARD® CORPORATION

7777 W. BLUEMOUND RD. P.O. BOX 13819 MILWAUKEE, WI 53213

Starlight Waltz

Violin

HARVEY S. WHISTLER

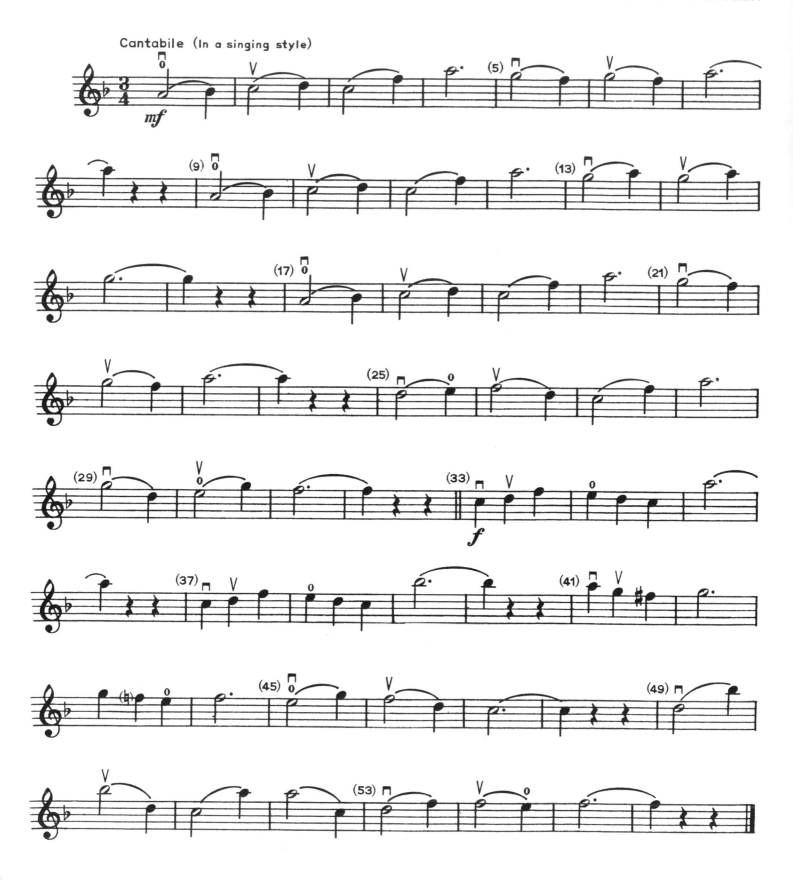

Copyright MCMLIV by Rubank, Inc., Chicago, Ill.
International Copyright Secured

Autumn Nocturne

Violin

HARVEY S. WHISTLER

To A Wild Rose

from Woodland Sketches

Violin

EDWARD MacDOWELL
Op. 51, No. 1

Evening Bells

Violin

HERMAN A. HUMMEL

Andante (Moving along; at a moderate rate of speed)

Prince Charming

RONDO

Violin

CHARLES DANCLA
Op. 123, No. 4

In A Clock Store

Violin

CHARLES J. ORTH

On Wings of Song

Violin

FELIX MENDELSSOHN

Cradle Song
(Wiegenlied)

Violin

MISKA HAUSER
Op. 11, No. 2

★ *Con sordino:* With the mute.   ★★ *Senza sordino:* Without the mute.

Christmas Serenade

Violin

Arr. Whistler-Hummel

SILENT NIGHT (Gruber)
Con affeto (With tenderness)

ADESTE FIDELIS (Traditional)
Devotamente (Devoutly)

JOY TO THE WORLD (Handel)
Maestoso (In a majestic manner)

Clown Dance

Violin

HERMAN A. HUMMEL

Scherzando (In a playful, happy mood)

* $\frac{3}{+}$ = Left hand pizzicato, plucking the string with the 3rd finger.

* $\frac{2}{+}$ = Left hand pizzicato, plucking the string with the 2nd finger.

Theme and Variation

Violin

CHARLES DANCLA
Op. 123, No. 7

On Wings of Song

FELIX MENDELSSOHN

Cradle Song

(Wiegenlied)

MISKA HAUSER
Op. 11, No. 2

Christmas Serenade

Arr. Whistler - Hummel

JOY TO THE WORLD (Handel)

Clown Dance

HERMAN A. HUMMEL

Theme and Variation

CHARLES DANCLA
Op. 123, No. 7